Stalked in Connecticut

poems

Martha Deborah Hall

Plain View Press
http://plainviewpress.net

1101 W. 34th Street, STE 404
Austin, TX 78705

Copyright © 2014 Martha Deborah Hall. All rights reserved under International and Pan-American Copyright Conventions. No part of this book may be reproduced or distributed in any form or by any means, or stored in a data base or retrieval system, without written permission from the author. All rights, including electronic, are reserved by the author and publisher.

ISBN: 978-1-63210-007-8
Library of Congress Control Number: 2014953417

Cover Art: *Snagged* by Linnea Gershenberg
Cover Design: Pam Knight

This is a work of fiction. Names, characters, places, and incidents either are the product of the author's imagination or are used fictitiously. Any resemblance to events, locales, or actual persons—living or dead—is entirely coincidental.

We Find Healing In Existing Reality

Plain View Press is a 36-year-old issue-based literary publishing house. Our books result from artistic collaboration between writers, artists, and editors. Over the years we have become a far-flung community of activists whose energies bring humanitarian enlightenment and hope to individuals and communities grappling with the major issues of our time—peace, justice, the environment, education and gender. This is a humane and highly creative group of people committed to art and social change. The poems, stories, essays, non-fiction explorations of major issues are significant evidence that despite the relentless violence of our time, there is hope and there is art to show the human face of it.

To Penny Lane,

who showed what friendship is all about.

Acknowledgements

Many of these poems appeared in the chapbook, titled "Interior Ransack", published by Finishing Line Press.

Contents

Part I: Interior Ransack — 9

Bang	11
Interior Ransack	12
Inner Binoculars	13
Trapped	14
C'est Moi	15
E Made Me Feel	16
Apart at the Seams	17
The Creep	18
In May at 2 PM	19
Sometimes I Felt Like…	20
News	21
Twitter This	22
A Peduncle	23
What Lies Do	24
Veggies	25
Down the Street	26
Like Teeth That Comb Through Your Hair	27
Got Glands?	28
Rumbles	29
Scatterings	30
Bile	31
When My Stalker Read in the Newspaper	32
Marginals	33
More Marginal Rants	34
Suspect	35
Let Me Release and Stomp on Their Lies, Then Bury Myself Someday on My Farm	36
My Pinocchio	37
As Nettlesome As	38

Part II: Stalked 39

Stalked	41
Once My Stalker Told Me…	42
Like a Rabbit…	43
On My Toe Tag…	44
One Word for It All	45
Skid Marks	46
Beneath the Weathervane…	47
My Inner Stadium	48
Voisins	49
Hey!	50
Christmas Tree Lane, Yeah, Right	51
Happy New Year	52
Zoonotics	53
Chigger Prize	54
Slop Jar	55
After 365 Days Times Three	56
Decision	57
On the Trail	58
Making Sense	59
Me With Crossed Arms Against…	60
Itchers	61
Deadheads	62
Funnel This	63
Night Thought	64
My House of Corrections	65

Part III: Cease and Desist　　67

Cease and Desist　　69
Once Gone　　70
Their Rat Trap　　71
Bye-Bye　　72
Divorce Van　　73
The Trash My Stalker Left　　74
Pesky Neighbors　　75
After My Stalker Moved Out of the Neighborhood　　76
Will You Forgive?　　77
Unlike Lilly Tomlin…　　78
Nits　　79
Inner Ear　　80
Seeing Red　　81
Advice　　82
My Ice Cream Poem　　83
Gotcha　　84
Blank Documents　　85
A Cinquain at 72　　86
Bridge to Sanity　　87
At My Digs　　89
Debbie Appleseed　　90
Time Balm　　91
In My Game　　92
Not Hers　　93
Gradually…　　94
In Tomorrow's Landscape　　95

About the Author　　97

Part I:
Interior Ransack

Bang

   1.
I took white gloves off, refused to smear them
with the excrement of your being. Symbolically,

I placed bullets upright on the shelf. "Shoot for
yourself against all maggots," I say. **Stalking is a crime**

of power and control. Not over me. Not on my watch.
You're the tick I've now contained, canned, and secured

in a jar. You've been boxed, burned, bagged, and banished.
It's my time to live, your time to die. Don't ever again try

to mess me up. Perhaps some day you'll see the big picture.
But ask me if I care.

   2.
Let me saunter down the road to the farm, recall dreams
left on my runways. Let me indulge in dark chocolate, my drug

of choice. Allow it to smooth and nurture inside me. Let me bob
in a rowboat on a warm July day, allowing wings of right

to soar in my skies. Let me hear the river on my morning walk
before I go home and complete daily chores. Allow me

to be as happy as a bear filled with honey. Let the gentle
feather of time at last recover.

Interior Ransack

It was like being left with no argument
for the existence of a higher power,
or being homeless after owning
a fourteen-room house, like a dream
that ends too soon, or a day
empty of awe, your interior void
of joy, like kitchen doors
without knobs, or a childhood
swimming hole covered in mud, or Elvis
unaccompanied by guitar, a man asleep
with his back to you, custody of a dead
parent, a sewing machine without thread,
a bird seen through binoculars, the wrong
end.

Inner Binoculars

Innately aware danger lurks.
See descent of a darker self.
I've no need for detective work.
I innately know danger lurks.
I'm victim of psychotic quirks.
Won't place my haunts upon a shelf.
Innately knowing danger lurks.
Fear mudslide to her darker self.

Trapped

She was like an alligator in my bathtub, a
lioness crouching on my porch, a cackling
hen under my windowsill, a fisher cat in my
closet, a red fox in my living room, maggots
in my laundry bin, a camel slurping dry my well,
elephant tusks stuck in my back, a rabid pit-
bull in my kitchen, a lizard in my sandbox, a
scorpion under my table, a flea sucking on my
right arm, a rat crawling in my attic, a stinking,
pink pig snorting in my barn. She brought out
the venomous, spitting cobra in the room called
me.

C'est Moi

abandoned,
banished,
caged,
dreary,
eradicated,
forlorned,
gaunt,
harrassed,
invaded,
jinxed,
knotted,
loathed,
mangled,
nothing,
ostracized,
pathetic,
quicksanded,
reclusive,
stigmatized,
targeted,
ulcerated
victimized,
wrecked,
x-rayed
yellowed,
zapped.

E Made Me Feel

anxiety-ridden
blighted
cyber-stalked
disenfranchised
exhausted
friendless
graceless
hated
indignant
jailed
key-holed
log-jammed
morphed
nutsy
ostracized
peace-less
quarantined
red-alerted
surveilled
terrorized
undermined
victimized
washed over
xanthic
yerked
zigzagged

Apart at the Seams

It hasn't been a tailored interface, my move toward age seventy. But I mended frayed cuffs, stitched unraveled hems, buttoned myself up to protect. This mender had been able to double back folded parts along the way. Some gatherings broke loose but on the whole, designs held like Velcro and zippers on winter jackets. Then stitches came undone. A needle pricked my fabric. Without thimble for the attack, pleats ripped away. Red buttons were thrown at my doorstep. Metal eyelets peered at comings and goings. My inner lining was under constant surveillance, my Singer depleted of golden thread.

The Creep

She yanks
out her cell phone,
aims in my direction,
pretends to talk, then snaps photo
of me.

In May at 2 PM

Splat! Splat!
I awaken.
Woman mumbling outside,
smearing my French door with rotten
pumpkin.

Sometimes I Felt Like...

A sink whose garbage disposal
would only swirl ends

of yellow summer squash
around its rim. Or rain water stopped

in the metal gutter, clogged
with once high flying

autumn leaves. Or a pond blocked
by a beaver dam. Or Niagara Falls

slowed to a trickle from lack
of rainfall. Or the Piscataqua River

that's been diverted for power.
Or the Atlantic shore at low tide

where everything had withdrawn
from the sun-filled beach.

News

I'm just an ordinary real estate broker and part time writer. No last name like Reagan, Letterman, or Foster. Just plain Hall. No national news coverage. Just a few press releases when my poetry books were published. But one doesn't have to be world famous to be the victim of another's obsessive behavior. My stalker craved attention, even if the only kind she could get was negative. She lied constantly and sometimes even called the police to report that *I* was stalking *her*. I guess it gave her some breaking, wake-up news in her boring life.

Twitter This

> *Well-known victims of stalking: Jennifer Aniston, Sandra Bullock, Justin Timberlake, Leann Rimes, Hilary Duff, Britney Spears, Madonna, and David Letterman*

Maybe if I were famous like them,
people would believe my profile
was as clean as theirs, that I
was the victim, not my stalker
as she now insists with her
fuzzy math. Maybe I could flick
her accusations from my shoulders,
like flies, fold them into the trash
like dirty paper picnic plates,
slough them off like a Band-Aid
that won't stick.

A Peduncle

A narrow stalk by which a tumor or polyp is attached

Balkers balk,
Caulkers caulk,
Chalkers chalk,
Gawkers gawk,
Moon walkers walk,
Shop talkers talk,
Sparrow Hawks hawk,
Squawkers squawk,
Stalkers accuse others of stalking.

What Lies Do

Untruths make us feel like broken wishbones,
prisoners of war, flashes in the pan, like elevators
stuck between floors. We drown in their swamps,
try to hide, keep separate company. Arrows shot
from their slings have landed in our hearts. Stuck
under the sink like rotting red potatoes, we feel
like boot-stomped rose petals in the pathway.
It's like we're internally infested with poison ivy.

Veggies

They're worm-holed potatoes,
stalks of carrots with decayed roots,
tomatoes bent in broken pots, beets
that exude soured red juice, turnips
decaying in their life's freezer,
soybeans in rancid butter, corn shorn
from cobs with unwashed hair,
moldy Brussels sprouts in a wet bag,
asparagus with bent, slimy stems,
cockroaches in my watering can.

Down the Street

Like one of the oldest apples at Mac's Orchard, she's marred with wormholes.

Like Teeth That Comb Through Your Hair

Each day old worms recrawl.
Spiders remend webs. Clock
hands scoot over yard arms.
Screwdrivers wrench through facades.
A bear survives without honey, exit
signs achieve their purpose. We all come
from a prison. Where is/was yours?

Got Glands?

A spider weaves its walls, spins in every room as it captures its prey.

Rumbles

Neighbor's
voicemail tells me
whacko's on premises.
Ever be freed from being held
hostage?

Scatterings

The car mechanic opened his fist to show me the steel nail, rimmed around the top in black paint, that had punctured my tire. A few weeks later I picked up identical nails placed in even rows behind my rear tires. Sprinkled similar nails met me underfoot as I stepped onto my brick patio last September. Then it fit together. I recalled my neighbor's barn sale: on one table a jar with pewter lid that I had opened, filled with half-inch nails scored around their tops with black paint.

Bile

Across
back sidewalk,
chalk-marked
footprints lead to my door.
Her riveted hatred flares again.
Knowing her similar patterns ignites
my nightmare marathon.

When My Stalker Read in the Newspaper

That I was a poet
She wrote a poem
and taped it to my door:
Ice cream
Ice cream
I scream

Marginals

M&Mers with chocolate melted on their hands,
SKORers without points,
Baby Ruthers with soured-milk rattles,
Butterfingers who drop life's truths,
KitKats who toy with others' feelings as they do mice,
Dove Bars with no mourning coos,
Her-she(y) narcissistics,
Snickers, traitors filled with nuts.

More Marginal Rants

They're changers with no agendas,
peaks of horses without whinnies,
sitters on elbows, non-getter-uppers,
cat walkers on wobbly terraces,
lip-readers without words of their own,
social climbers in mothballed suits,
Gucci baggers with empty wallets,
robins with fleas in their nests,
watchers of others who do life's weeding,
cows who moo, "You act first,
then in the hay I will wallow."

Suspect

Wearing
limey, dirty
vest, on new motor bike,
he turns into Welfare Office
to prey.

Let Me Release and Stomp on Their Lies, Then Bury Myself Someday on My Farm

A refugee from childhood, how would I know if fairy tales or stories resonate with me if no one ever read them to me? Maybe every so often I "heard" from the Bible at "sleepy-time," but I still cringe if someone refers to Paul the Dauntless. I was never read to from "Sleeping Beauty," "The "13th Godmother at the Christening," "Chicken Little," "Goldilocks and the Three Bears," or "The Snow Queen," so can't/don't/won't relate. One thing I do know is I am not an example of a person "who cries wolf." I can't seem to write a fairy tale. I've tried. I'd like to throw in the trash children's books I've read lately at our public library or local bookstores. Dump in there also large portions of so-called "music" dissed to us at concerts, on radios and CDs. I will fight for new moose/mouse crossing signs on our highways and will stomp-rage against the storage of nuclear waste in our oceans. **Have you ever heard of anything so crazy, stupid and irresponsible?** How about if you become the object of someone else's besmirched, seething obsessions? "UH-OH, WATCH OUT" might be the title of my non-fractured, non-fairy tale truth book. They could write a non-fiction one, title it: "GOOD PEOPLE WE'VE BESMIRCHED."

My Pinocchio

A mean,
maligning,
malevolent,
malicious,
moronic,
mistaken,
murderous,
malignant,
mealy-mouthed,
menace
with monstrous nose.

As Nettlesome As

having a mosquito buzz your bedroom in the middle of the night, or having the cake all gone once your turn comes. As bothersome as a baby who keeps dropping his binky, or a needy neighbor who wants to chat every time you come home. As pesky as a dandelion reappearing each year because you haven't killed the taproot. As irritating as having a flat tire in the middle of a bike race or being on the pier without a hook for your line. As annoying as when the toaster pops a waffle on the floor or when an unseen snake slithers and startles. As disagreeable as fourteen days of rain in a row. As vexatious as when you shout truth from your heart and no one hears.

Part II:
Stalked

Stalked

Most women are stalked
by men. Not me. Wouldn't
you know it? Just
my luck. Was she
interested in me
sexually? Probably not.
Just a committed
crazy willing to go
to any length
to bother me,
knowing she had
made me
lie in my bed
in night
sweats.

Once My Stalker Told Me...

that she came from a together-broken home,
that her father had been a molester, a sexual cobra,
and her mother a bi-polar vulture. I asked her
what she thought she herself had been.
A bunny, she said, but not anymore.

Like a Rabbit...

Stunned by a bee-bee gun but breathing, I lie on my ground and then start kicking. After all, aren't we taught in America: we don't sit on the sideline, when you drink someone else's poison you pay the price, you shouldn't have a normal discussion when someone has beaten the crap out of you? Didn't you hear yesterday's hopes may have been made of salt but tomorrow's can be made of granite? Even if you're in the back seat you can chase your dreams as Alan Shepherd did. Don't let mourning return to town. Failure is not failing, it's not trying. A twenty-year-old knife can still do an excellent job. These statements swirl into a lifetime where old age spots aren't a source of embarrassment. I have ice-blood in my veins at the age of seventy. I may have heard the weather five minutes ago and two minutes later have forgotten what was said, but I know once I turn the oven on, the chocolate chip cookies will start baking. My footprints may show crooked in the snow but this sun-flake's head steers in the right direction. Bellow out who you are to any protagonist, store complacency in your life on the shelf. I am I. Who are you?

On My Toe Tag...

Please inscribe (if you have enough room) the following: Don't say I never lived; I went there like a BB gun. On the beefy menu bowl of things I did and owned in spirit, state that I supported laws in favor of helmets. If you've done away with the elephants in your living room, be certain to use leftover ivory tusks for weapons against potential predators or for stripping the bark from trees that get in your way. If you sink under water after a risky dive, kick your feet, flap your arms, forge upward and then breathe. Unzip your beliefs, let them air in our universe, own and support them. Let a key unlock your childhood bedroom door; bring the teddy bear left on your bunk bed a jar of honey. If interior scars won't heal, give them air, some time; seek help from others, you will come through. Don't forget to say "hi" every morning to your sugar jar. Give your accounts and beliefs high energy, even if some are flawed. Don't let others stomp or flail on your dreams, your you. Before I departed I hope you read I wanted to be fed marmalade and Land O Lakes butter on Pepperidge Farm rye bread. That way I'll be able to go out in a final, happy coma. Remember, the quicker I get to home plate at the end, the better my chances are of a final, successful win. But most of all after I go, don't forget to deliver my last words to them: "FUCK YOU."

Sign it: Tippy-Toe-not!!!

One Word for It All

Fuckie-fuckie-fuck,
Fuckie-fuckie-fuck-fuck-fuck,
Fuckie-fuckie-fuck

Skid Marks

Traffic
jams on life's high-
ways, dung-infested back
roads is where I ended up, thanks
to them.

Beneath the Weathervane...

On a dull-dark splayed metal table,
a black crow with black beak, black
talons, black fountain pen, an aluminum
cup with black handle and frame, a Gucci
watch with black leather strap, a black
briefcase filled with my written statements
documenting your bi-polar behavior, black
memories of your dung.

My Inner Stadium

One woman in twelve will be stalked in her lifetime.
 — 2000 Department of Justice study

At the goalpost near the high school football field, an empty Virgil beer bottle is splattered with vomit. Nearby, exterior locker walls are smeared with graffiti expressing anger at victorious opponents. Discarded popcorn bags lay soaked on stadium benches. No one hawks hot dogs. Loudspeakers are turned off. Emptied balloons sag on strings on fences. A scoreboard reads 13 to 0 in favor of the away team. A player's unwanted obsession with me has intimidated my team. She keeps throwing completed passes at my interior scoreboard. Allowing myself no timeout, I must scramble again to score touchdowns on my behalf, be my own cheerleader, prance forward in my marching band, even if future odds of stopping her are against me. So I'll dust myself off, restart my game. As I stand here alone on the field, a black snake slithers into the end zone.

Voisins

I don't,
but if I did

pray, I'd ask,
with moral

certitude and
any ounce left

of the seventy-
one-year-old

girl power
in my being,

to have
these snakes

coiled, boxed,
and relocated.

Hey!

At 5 AM I had just stepped out of my condo and onto my front path for a morning walk in Lakeside Village. She sped into the complex driving at about 60 MPH in a black van and came close to hitting me. The speed limit sign here reads 10 MPH and warns "Watch for pedestrians and small animals." Oh well!! I motioned to her to slow down. She flipped me the bird. In the suicide right front seat, dragging on a cigarette, sat her teen age son. They were delivering morning copies of the daily newspapers to various units here. This winter I witnessed her take too quick a turn into the driveway and she creamed her Buick's still-duct-taped fender, scraping and splitting off a piece of the granite block at the entrance. Vroom, vroom, she stormed this morning as radio music blared. On her way out, she gave me the middle finger again. Whatever!!!

Christmas Tree Lane, Yeah, Right

Like a Subaru Forester poised to push through the snow, I got up at five a.m. so I could get to the hospital by seven. Breakfast, shower, dress, and I'm on my way. I prance out the door, bundled in down. Smeared on my garage window and around the outside of the keyhole is excrement. I go to the President of the Board, asking, "What shall I do this time?" He says he'll call the police. I head off to my appointment. I remind myself that just because a person steams out of a church parking lot doesn't mean they have the right of way. Devils can move out in life and saints move in but not in this case. I ask others, "What can possibly go on in the mind of this type of person?" "This is how they get a fix," one neighbor says. I think it's how they validate themselves. I don't come apart externally, but on the inside I feel like a caged, tortured gorilla. Another friend recommends mediation. But how does one mediate with a crazy? Shall I pack my suitcase, leave these insults in an attic trunk, or commence to collect my due? In my mind I want to go row alone on the Charles. But, scrappy at seventy, I finally decide. I'll keep blowing the whistle until somebody hears.

Happy New Year

I ring it in by going to bed around nine.
Soft wind on the pane lulls me to sleep.
My down blanket, by definition, comforts.
The first goal-task of the New Year
is to take a one-mile walk. Out the door
at five in the morning I see her staring
from her window. I ask myself:
MGWAM (My God, what about me?)

Zoonotics

The five a.m. alarm roars. I jump out of bed, throw white longies on under my maroon and black warm-up suit, even wear a bra this morning along with my yellow and black visor, and new Dollar Store pinky fleece mittens. Set for my morning walk, I storm to my front door but wait: They are out there. In the four years I've lived here, this is the first time I've seen them at this hour. They're loading the black SUV with a saggy looking mattress and lime green wicker chair seen previously on the porch. Perhaps the divorce gossip is true. He is done with her and she must be out of their condo by the first of November. But, as is always the case with these loony birds, "The Blessing is next to the Wound." Neighbors tell me the hawks say I'm responsible for their divorce, just as I'm the one who supposedly threw rotten pumpkin on my slider, who stole my door keys off my front hall table, the one who threw a handful of nails behind my car tires, the one who smeared my garage door and window with excrement, the one who supposedly socked her, the one who "swears at her every time I see her," the one who stalked her when she-they were the ones who came out and stalled my freedom with maligning gossip about other neighbors every time I stepped out of my door. I'm the one who was "responsible" for their undoing: her fourth divorce, his second. Here is my reaction: Did anyone of those four husbands ever try to get professional psychiatric help for her? Has anyone else taken a look at her previous real estate tax delinquencies on three other houses she owned? I've been a real estate broker for forty-five years and have never witnessed anything like this irresponsible behavior. What lies within her core? Why did she send birthday cards to her siblings on which she wrote death threats to herself and forged my initials. Why was my mail tampered with on another occasion? A tinge of sadness for them leaked from my essence, but then I pulled hundreds of festooning pages of court documents from my files on which I had to spend thousands of dollars of hard-earned money to defend myself against their lies, money I wanted my children and grand-children to enjoy someday. My answer to the question, "Was I right?" is Yes!!!!!!!!! And I want them both to get the fuck out of here.

Chigger Prize

You win
my life award.
Thanks for deep-cut wrinkles
that healing hands of time will soothe.
Bullshit.

Slop Jar

If alive, my twin would have held my hand, slapped you in your scuzzy face.

After 365 Days Times Three

Christmas cards taped to my refrigerator have been tossed. **Sorry if one of them was yours.** I indulged in New Year's Eve. The "healing hands of time" didn't. The herding of once immersed forgiveness has been sucked down my drains. Any further apologies *for things I didn't do in the first place* are impossible. It's opening night at my theater. I'm on center stage. The little girl with white gloves praying in the first row pew has been resurrected as a nuclear bomb.

Decision

Over Labor Day weekend, I closed
the cabin, stored pink sheets, folded
up cots, placed porch chairs inside,
then took a last walk around the pond.
Waves lapped good-bye. I dropped a stone
where the baby duck had fallen
victim to a weasel, all that was left of it
fluff, and I knew I would never
be like that, determined
now to call a lawyer
first thing in the morning.

On the Trail

I'm not Sam Spade, but I don't need a color coded map to lead me to the protagonist. I need a judge to end my holocaust and cast a decision in my favor against her. It blows my mind that she constantly intrudes my privacy. I can't prove she's the one who stole my front door key. She often comes out when most people in the complex are at work or are gone to tend their daily chores. I've only seen her out at 7:30 in the morning once in my life. Someone in the Complex told me she sleeps past noon. Since I have different working hours than most, it seems I'm a solitary witness a lot of the time to her goings on. But I didn't see her take my front door key. Nor did I see her take my garage door key—the one I used to leave in the electric slot. I know that was foolish, but you try going to your car with a briefcase, a bag of garbage, books and/or movies that need returning to the library, dry cleaning or a letter that needs mailing and then have to dig into that briefcase for your garage door key. It's annoying to have to put everything on the ground to search. But now it, too, is missing from its slot. Last week I went to put a chair in my storage. Someone nicely clamped the lock that I had purposely left open so I could gain access. Who is the meddler? I think I innately know. What do you think?

Making Sense

Instead of shelling out hard-earned money for a lawyer to deal with this mail-tampering, "Dime Store Talc" stalker, I could've paid my grandchild's future college tuition, or put a sizable down payment on a second condo. I could've purchased a new Saab, five "Evenings in Paris," some shares of Exxon stock, or a motorboat which my children could have used to water ski on their favorite lake. I could've paid for a living room of "Woodhue" vintage antiques, or four years of heating bills. The scents she wore, "Poison," "Scandal," and "Shocking," left me with a lifetime worth of payments toward unlocking the chains of emotional stress she caused. But I must remember, regret and anger can do you in, can make you dance to a "Blue Waltz."

Me With Crossed Arms Against...

bluffers, bullies, buts, blots, blizzards,
buffoons, blockheads, blemishes, bull
shitters, blights, blood suckers. I'm blameless.

Itchers

Today
N.H.P.R.
spoke of the millions killed
by the plague. Stated cause was fleas,
like you.

Deadheads

They were gapers, non-enterprising dullards who sat as others weaved.

Funnel This

I'm not a peckerhead, an orange head,
a jug head, or a troubled soul. I may dress
like Ronny McDonalds' granny, but I make
mincemeat of unfair transgressions, let you
know when you're a P.I.T.A. So filter this
and listen: Leave me alone. Get it?

Night Thought

Sirens
from ambulance
shriek in her yard. Police
cars soon follow. Is neighbor dead?
I hope.

My House of Corrections

I'd stand
in line to see
your execution, keep
my name on the waiting list for
decades.

Part III:
Cease and Desist

Cease and Desist

Opened
fists by my side.
Rotten pumpkin throwing
blitzes terminated now. No
lawyers.

Once Gone

Rotten yellow squash no longer thrown.
No nails found outside my garage.
I took her on, confronted
her demonic being,
ignored her dribble,
finally won.
The pig moved
out of
town.

Their Rat Trap

Snow melts
in the driveway
of my Coldwell Banker
office. MLS download says
it's closed.

Bye-Bye

Not a
single person
helps them move out. No one
throws a farewell going away
party.

Divorce Van

As she drives off in her loaded, black rogue Ford, I clap.

The Trash My Stalker Left

A camera with broken lens.
A soiled, O.J. Simpson styled glove.
A clock with its minute hand stuck.
An empty perfume bottle: Hugo Boss
Deep Red. The book, **From Here
to Eternity,** where hopefully
this mad woman has gone forever.

Martha Deborah Hall

Pesky Neighbors

Like dandelions, whose taproots produce from one to ten annoying stems each, they won't go away unless weeded. The puffy semen-eggs can produce over a hundred future weeds. They love to embed themselves near roadsides, surround favorite crimson maples, and inject themselves near placid summer ponds. Their bright yellow heads can sometimes mislead. They root in the backyard of your universe, in nearby hayfields, in the hedges near vintage stone walls. They intrude through cracks in unused tennis courts, immerse themselves in brick patios leading to your pool. So get rid of them. Don a plastic accordion-folded rain hat for digging them in the rain. Bring a tissue or napkin to wipe perspiration, the longest screw driver in your tool kit to dig up their roots, a metal stool you can spin around on for your attacks. Wear white rubber gloves to daintily match the fluffs, wrap a plastic bag around a pail's perimeter, march with seeded endorphins in your outfields as to war. Dig out life's festering stems. Be the tufted, perennial fruit that was once called you.

After My Stalker Moved Out of the Neighborhood

For months I've dug up soil, shoveled it back, waltzed four steps, then stopped. Now I sleep peacefully, no nightmares to wake me screeching. I get up at dawn, toss anxiety medicine in the trash, serve myself French Vanilla coffee from a purple finch embossed mug, sit at my peach-colored table, and gaze at a bouquet of pink dianthus from my garden. I take a long hot shower, get dressed, and apply **L'Oréal Plush Velvet** on my smiling lips. I grab my Gucci bag, go out to my silver convertible, and put the top down, planning to take my grandkids out to lunch and to the park. On my way out, I pass my former neighbor's house with its puce-colored, peeling clapboards. In my mind I throw my "old blues" in the rusty, metal bucket sitting on the porch.

Will You Forgive?

No,
Anny,
Nein,
Nyat,
Na,
Non,
Nun,
Mam,
Ba,
Poi-e
Ne,
Neyn,
Ket,
Nope,
Nie,
Maan,
Nyi,
Ko,
Nana,
Nej,
Naw,
No way,
Nee,
Nenni,
Nesats,
Nem,
Naaga,
Nau,
Nit.
Get it?

Unlike Lilly Tomlin...

> *Forgiving is giving up all of the past.*
> — Lilly Tomlin

I shall never forgive you.
Nothings,
you are smidgeons,
ping pong balls, ***ping pong pings***.
Drunkards of your party, you learned:
Not me.

Nits

On the radio this morning, a story about a guy who had been diagnosed with terminal brain cancer. Knowing he was going to die, he made out a short bucket list:

Go to Jiggles Bar and Grill.
Parachute out of an airplane.
Return to Jiggles. **He knew he'd like it.**

I turned the radio off, decided I really didn't care if this dude lived or died. But what would your wishes be? My sister died twelve years ago today, almost to the minute. Some of her ashes are buried at Westview Cemetery. I'll be buried in the plot next to her when my turn comes but, in the meantime, I need to be forgiven for what a friend has termed my "eradication list," those people one might like to see go bye-bye—so to speak. I really do hate three people; others I may dislike but these three I detest. The first one is Justin Bieber. I watched him in court on TV yesterday, snottily excusing his despicable behavior in front of the judge, his defense attorney, and the prosecutor. He's supposed to be setting an example for others. He's famous. He's wasting the world's time with his abrasive, self-indulgent, egotistical, stupid, boring, inept, extraneous excuses for his behavior. What a role model. Yeah right!!! He has been clicked/extricated/eradicated from my life, never to receive another chance—not that I ever gave him one in the first place. Scram, Justin, you're a ***fait accompli***. The other two that I'd like to symbolically eradicate from the face of this earth are code-named "Straddles" and "Quarter-incher." Only a few people know of whom I speak. I'll probably be chronically infested with memories of their behavior. But there's medicine to remove lice from one's being, and forgiving them is not in the mix. There's still a great deal of itching left, but I think I'll ultimately be medicated by time and will be able to eradicate them before the day comes when I say to my sister, "Move over, please. I'm on my way there."

Inner Ear

The devil communicated with me. This time there was no evil in the message. "You always do hurt the ones you love," it said. I thought I had good reason. But I did hurt them. I got on my knees last week. In my heart, I beckoned certain people and told them I was sorry. I had coffined good behavior, had been under unbearable anxiety, but it was no excuse for my verbal tirades against family members. I begged them to forgive me. I have finally been able to shred old, stress-soaked bandages. Fog seemed to clear from the pond outdoors. Sunshine flooded the room.

Seeing Red

It's time to reapply strawberry lipstick, revamp wasted years, reclaim life's stairways. Resume repumping of life's ventricles. Re-release silenced lullabies of love, revive retired hugs of old. Recapture love that steered away, recapitulate it in your heart, revalidate its everlasting glory, regroup thought processes that strangled its existence. Rekindle goodness with loving behavior. Retrieve its buried essence, remove the tears, and reopen your arms to it. Let roses replenish in sparkling gardens. Reconstruct picket fences, fling wide white gates. Reopen closed hands. Replace angst by repeating heart rhythm strands of words and actions that resound with, "I love you."

Advice

To me:

Show what you believe in by action.
Bang piano notes across the room.
Waltz in your cornfields.
Learn from your errors.
Go for up!
Sow your artistic seeds.
If yesterday's page was empty, fill today's with love.
If former hopes dissolved in salt, carve today's in granite.
Stand on your stand.

To her:

Go jump in the lake.

My Ice Cream Poem

She was like strawberry ice cream
festering with e-coli, rum raisin
drooling down your chin, or **Crow**
sorbet that caws and melts, a sour
Klondike Bar left too long on a counter,
or a French Vanilla sundae without any sun.
Now that she's gone, I can finally enjoy
a **Time Out** float, walk down Main Street
without the stress of being followed or watched,
sit on a park bench with no **Caramel Chaos**.

Gotcha

Yesterday, out on my morning walk,
I bumped into an old neighbor.
In our tight conversation
she said she was told that
"Quarter-incher" sat
on the toilet
whenever
he pee-
peed.

Blank Documents

That's what you are, have been, were, always will be forevermore, two blanks.

A Cinquain at 72

Life's full
of bad hair days,
ongoing births and deaths.
Get out from under those covers,
then live.

Bridge to Sanity

In my golden years, I'm going
72 MPH, the same numeral
as my age. I'm just grateful
for friends and family
who helped me live
through my nightmares
one second at a time,
and to carry on
with a full tank of gas.

Somewhat healed, I can look back
and write of what I've learned.
Flags are finally raised again.
I fair well. But what about when
I was severely chapped on the interior?
Who stood by? Who did not?

One day as I came home
from a late afternoon walk,
my stalker charged toward me
with her snapping mutt on a leash.
I kept moving out of her way
until I literally had to stop
or walk into the pond to escape her.
I screamed for help, hoping
a neighbor would hear me.
Thankfully, Elsie was home.
She came out verbally swinging.

Later, when we were alone
and had a chance to settle down,
she told me she'd been about to go
to the drugstore when she heard me
yelling for help. Then she grinned
and asked me if I would
like her to pick me up a tube
of anti-fungal cream. We both laughed
until tears streamed down our faces.

She was a true friend. Other people
hid under their rugs with no idea
how isolated and cut off I felt.
To the friends and family
who supported and stood by me,
I'm eternally indebted. They helped me
rebuild my bridge to sanity
one piece of steel at a time.

At My Digs

Coffee
table book life
now. Snow-banked happenings
commence to melt. I am in my
right here.

Debbie Appleseed

Embedded in this red delicious apple were seeds splayed when once thrown in anger as a graveled snowball against a concrete wall.

"Splat," it screamed. But one seed dug into spring's rich earth, rejuvenated and persevered. Relaxing and reflecting in its orchard some years later on a fine April day after these terrifying experiences settled in, the seed sat and wrote this poem:

Stink Bugs...
Go snap, stop, cease, desist,
send yourselves away, you scabs,
shits, skunks, scraps, smelly slobs,
you scroungy snots, you staring splats
in my April breeze. Squat on your sins,
your lies, you scorpions. Scram for once
and for all, you bi-polar stalking snag.

Time Balm

Sweet breeze caresses the windowsills.
Letters cease. Phone calls terminate.
Shit. This is so refreshing.
They had been precursors
sewn in threads of hate,
burst Pyrex pots
of coffee
thrown at
me.

In My Game

Losses: None.

Wins:

Alligator jaws moved south.
TAT Fly Paper sucked in old dead insects.
Pipe cleaners unclogged internal strain drains.
I don my little cowgirl vest of old for fun.
Pink ballerina slippers adorn memories.
12-ounce cups of hot chocolate with whipped cream soothe me daily.
I weigh in right on the cusp on my metal scale.
Multi-colored wooden eggs charm my brick patio birdbath.
I store fleece jackets in an attic bin.
I give a furlough to Dr. Nancy, my sleep therapist.
Former daydreams march into achieved goals.
Joie dans ma vie.
My Venetian blinds are in a permanent up position.

Not Hers

Mine, the only footprints in this New England snow, I follow them home.

Gradually...

My home becomes mine again. I open
my drapes, begin to believe in goodness
once more, entering the paradise
of sunshine outside my door, the Sunday
paper on the patio, the geese soaring over
the pond. I take a deep breath, am still.

In Tomorrow's Landscape

No more rain will fall.
Only light will glance against my newly Windex-ed windows.
Murphy's Law proves to be untrue.
Valentine's Day is around the corner.
Spring and I shall soon have an untethered pow-wow.
Meadow grass will be sown, grown, and mown.
Christmas bulbs frozen in the birdbath will soon defrost.
New keys will open former jammed interior portals.
Summer will glide in.

About the Author

Martha Deborah Hall is the author of eleven books of poetry: seven full-length collections, *The Closing, The Opening* (WordTech Communications), five from Plain View Press, *The Weight of Light, Two Grains in Time, My Side of the Street, Inside Out* (nominated for a Pushcart Award in 2011), and *Heading Toward Silver Dust*, and *White Out: Poems on Drugs and Suicide* (D-N Publishing), along with four chapbooks, *The Garbo Reels* (Pudding House Press), *Abandoned Gardens* (winner of the 2005 John and Miriam Morris Chapbook contest at The Alabama State Poetry Society), *Silver Dust: Poems on Aging* (Indigo Mosaic Press), and *Mooring Lines* (Finishing Line Press). Her manuscripts have been finalists in contests by Sarabande Books, the Kathryn A. Morton Prize in Poetry, the Vernice Quebodeaux "Pathways" Poetry Prize, and the Concrete Wolf Chapbook contest (twice).

Honored by the New Hampshire Poet Laureate to be one of NH's featured poets on his web site, her work has also appeared in such journals as *Bellowing Ark, Common Ground Review, Las Cruces, Old Red Kimono, Tale Spinners, Tapestries, The Poet's Touchstone,* and *Watch the Eye*. Holding degrees from Ohio Wesleyan University and Columbia University, she is a member of the Academy of American Poets, The Poetry Society of New Hampshire, and the Monadnock Writers' Group.

Martha Deborah Hall
135 Amherst St., Unit 6
Amherst, NH 03031
(603) 672-0106
debhall1@myfairpoint.net
http://marthadeborahhall.com

www.ingramcontent.com/pod-product-compliance
Lightning Source LLC
Chambersburg PA
CBHW052109070526
44584CB00017B/2400